Preparing for Fatherhood

....

Deepak Reju

New Growth Press

WWW.NEWGROWTHPRESS.COM

New Growth Press, Greensboro, NC 27404
www.newgrowthpress.com

Cover Design: Faceout Books, faceoutstudio.com
Typesetting: Lisa Parnell, lparnell.com

ISBN: 978-1-942572-16-9 (Print)
ISBN: 978-1-942572-17-6 (eBook)

Library of Congress Cataloging-in-Publication Data
Reju, Deepak, 1969–
  Preparing for fatherhood / Deepak Reju.
    pages cm
  ISBN 978-1-942572-16-9 (print) — ISBN 978-1-942572-17-6
(ebook)
 1. Fatherhood—Religious aspects—Christianity. 2. Fathers—
Religious life. I. Title.
  BV4529.17.R45 2015
  248.8'421—dc23

                                              2015002679

Printed in Canada

22 21 20 19 18 17 16 15   1 2 3 4 5

For me the big news came just outside of our local pharmacy, as my wife and I were pulling into the parking lot. She looked at me and said, "Are you coming in?"

"Yes. Why?"

"Because if you are coming in, then you need to know that I'm buying a pregnancy test. I think I'm pregnant."

That quickly, my whole life changed.

The moment any man realizes he is about to become a father marks a pivotal shift in his life. What is ahead for a first-time dad is both remarkable and scary. Are you ready for the big change? Are you wondering what it will take to be a good father? And how will you handle the transition into fatherhood?

Changes at the Beginning

As you face the prospect of becoming a father, you might assume that the only person who will change in the next nine months is your baby's mother. Certainly her physical changes are very noticeable, but she's not the only one going through changes. You will be sorting through a lot of different thoughts and emotions as well. Here are a few you will likely face:

Fear and Worry. If you are like most men, when you find out that you are going to be a dad for the first time, you will have plenty of worries and concerns.

Uncertainty and unfamiliarity usually scare people. You may think

> *Will I be able to do this? I don't know the first thing about kids. I've never changed a diaper before . . .*

> *How can we afford this? What's this going to do to our budget? What if my wife gets sick? What if she can't work anymore?*

> *When I was growing up, my home life was a wreck. I don't want to turn out like my father.*

> *I've heard you don't get much sleep. What if I get impatient, short-tempered, and angry?*

> *Will our baby be healthy? What if the baby is not healthy? What will I do?*

Joy and Excitement. Mixed with the worries, there is also a lot of joy. Hopefully when you heard the news, you were excited about becoming a father. And even if the news took you by surprise, you have some time to adjust to your new reality. Maybe you will start to dream about what it will be like to be a dad. Perhaps you are thinking about Little League games, throwing a baseball in the backyard, teaching your child about Star Wars, fishing, or shooting guns. Maybe you'll coach your kids in soccer, join them for tea parties with baby dolls, or get away together for weekend camping trips. Whatever your hopes or dreams, the possibility of having a son or daughter to share life with is thrilling.

Anger, Confusion, or Distress. Maybe you did not plan to become a father, or at least, not this soon. In your mind this was a big mistake. Perhaps you are not married to the mother of your unborn child. Whatever the situation, your initial reaction was nothing like the glee-filled moments you see in Hollywood movies. If this is you, take some time to think through why you responded the way you did. Is there a secret fear lurking beneath your anger? Maybe you're afraid of the cost of having a child, or that you'll become like your own father. Recognize that God doesn't make mistakes when it comes to babies or anything else (Psalm 139:13–16). He placed this child into your life, he is calling you to the responsibility of fatherhood, and he will provide what you need to do the job (2 Peter 1:3).

A Sense of the Surreal. You can't believe this is actually happening to you. Your wife still looks the same. Nothing else in your life has changed just yet, but you know change is coming. Some days, it's still a little hard to believe.

Amid the thoughts and concerns running through your mind, you might wonder, *Will I be a good father?* How will you become the man and father you would like to be? What would it look like from God's perspective to become a father? The one who made you and knows you better than you know yourself will guide you through the ups and downs, joys and challenges of becoming a dad.

Note to Single Dads

Even if you are not married to the mother of your child, this minibook is for you. Of course I don't know the ins and outs of your particular situation, but I do know that your child needs an involved, loving, faithful father. Regardless of your relationship with the mother, never forget how much your child needs you. Most of this minibook can be applied to your situation, even if you aren't currently married.

A Wonderful Gift

Sometimes children are viewed as an inconvenience, but God's perspective is different. He describes children as a reward from him (Psalm 127:3–5). To have many children—"a quiver full of them"—is not an inconvenience, but a blessing.

As with everything else in life, Jesus shows us the way forward by his perspective on the youngest of children.

> People were bringing little children to Jesus
> to have him touch them, but the disciples
> rebuked them. When Jesus saw this, he was
> indignant. He said to them, "Let the little
> children come to me, and do not hinder
> them, for the kingdom of God belongs to
> such as these. Truly I tell you, anyone who
> will not receive the kingdom of God like a
> little child will never enter it." And he took

the children in his arms, put his hands on
them and blessed them. (Mark 10:13–16)

While the disciples tried to keep the children and
their parents away from Jesus, he welcomed them.
Much like our world today, the culture in first-century
Jerusalem didn't value children. Yet Jesus saw children as having immense importance and value. He
didn't consider their helplessness a problem, but an
example to us all. Children show us how we must be
in our relationship with our heavenly Father (v. 15)—
forever dependent on him (Acts 17:28). During
another conversation, Jesus told his disciples that who-
ever welcomes children in Jesus's name is actually wel-
coming God (Mark 9:36–37).

Stop and think about your attitude toward children, and especially your child. Do you see a child as
an inconvenience and someone who would get in the
way of your plans? Parenting is not a hobby, something you do in your extra time, and children are not
a possession, something you "own" like a car or house.
Children are image-bearers of God (Genesis 1:26–27)
and worshipers. They will spend their life either wor-
shiping God or something else (just like you). Your
greatest responsibility as a parent is to point your child
to God—the one who loved them and gave his life for
them (Romans 5:8).

The picture that emerges from what God says
about children is that they are to be treasured, valued,

respected, loved, and cherished. The great sacrifices that parents make for their kids are not just because they love their kids (which they do), but because they love the great God who entrusted these kids to them.

Fatherhood Changes You

Becoming a father is a great opportunity for you to grow in faith and love—the two most important things in life. You will find that parenting takes more sacrifice, time, energy, and love than you have available. Finding that out is a good thing because it will force you to go to God for the help you need to love your child well. Early on, in those sleepless nights when you don't have any strength, God will teach you to depend on him. As your child grows, he or she will ask questions that you don't know how to answer. The questions will stretch you, so you'll have to grow in your knowledge of God and the Bible to be able to teach your child. When your child goes in a wrong direction, you'll come to see that you can't change his or her heart. Only God can.

I heard one father say, "God used fatherhood to make me face up to my self-centeredness." Marriage begins that process, as two broken people learn to give grace to one another despite each other's many faults. As a husband, you learn to give up the dreams of doing what you want when you want and start considering your wife's needs before your own. Fatherhood will continue that process. Every day you'll be called to give up your life for your children. If you accept the challenge, you will find that God is using parenthood to save you from self-centeredness and to make you into the man that God intended for you to be all along.

Our world pictures a real man as a guy who is strong, powerful, athletic, confident, and macho. Picture Sylvester Stallone, face beaten in, standing in the ring with hands raised. Contrast these images with what will be required of you as a new father—not just strength and confidence, but tenderness. Your calling is to be *both a lion and a lamb*. You need strength and confidence to lead your family, but also a sweet tenderness to care for a helpless, newborn infant. Jesus exemplified this in his life. He had the courage to stand up to the religious elite (Luke 5:22–24, 33; 6:2) who hated him, and he was also willing to give his life as a sacrifice for our sake (Hebrews 12:2). Throughout his life, he cared for the weak and sick (Matthew 4:23–25; Luke 10:25–37) and set an example of service and self-sacrifice (John 13).

Jesus is the perfect picture of servant-hearted leadership for fathers to emulate. In the days ahead, becoming a dad will demand that you grow more like Jesus in strength, confidence, and kindheartedness. But God doesn't ask you to do that on your own. As you ask for help in the moments when you would rather do anything else than take care of a baby, Jesus will help you. Sometimes, especially for guys, asking for help is the last thing we want to do. But there is no shame in going to your Father in heaven for the help you need. You don't have to pretend before God that you know more and are stronger than you really are. He already knows how needy you are, and he wants you to ask for help to love your family daily, hourly, and for many years to come.

Your Wife Needs You

As you change, your wife will also change. Sure, her body will change as the baby grows in her womb, but there is more. She's probably wanted to be a mom, and now she's finally getting the baby she's wanted. But the hard work and sacrifice required will also be difficult for her—really too difficult to get through without your help. Through pregnancy, delivery, and the first few months of postpartum recovery, what will be most pronounced, and possibly new for your relationship, is how frail and weak your wife will be. It starts with morning sickness. Sometimes there are complications with the pregnancy. Certainly she will be exhausted. She's stressed about all the changes. After the birth she'll be sleep-deprived and short-tempered, with her emotions in turmoil from exhaustion and hormonal changes.

Sounds fun, doesn't it? This might seem like a recipe for disaster. But in God's world our weakness is an opportunity for him to show himself sufficient to help us through every difficult moment that comes our way (2 Corinthians 12). Seeing the power of God on display in weakness and sacrificing yourself for the good of your wife and child—these are the things that make life rich, meaningful, and full. This is not a disaster waiting to happen, but an opportunity for you. You get to be a father who uses his strength to care for his wife and baby while they are weak and needy (Mark 10:42–45).

Though there are many changes to come in the months and years after your child's birth, there are things that will remain unchanged. Your primary goal in life will still be to love God and love others (Mark 12:28–34). What God requires from us doesn't change with our circumstances. In a way, that should make your life refreshingly simple. God's law of love helps to narrow your focus to what's most important. You get to figure out what love looks like in this new phase of life. As you enter fatherhood, you can be certain that love will be defined as denying yourself (Mark 8:34); giving up your own plans and goals so you can help your wife and child (Ephesians 5:25–33; 6:4); and being patient with your wife during her weakness (1 Peter 3:7).

Get Your Priorities Straight: Husband First; Dad Second

With all this talk about parenting, it's important to not forget about your marriage. Always keep in mind that the strength of your parenting is rooted in the strength of your relationship. The stronger your marriage, the stronger your parenting will be. In the first few months of parenting, it will certainly feel like everything is revolving around your new baby. And rightfully so—you and your wife are making a big adjustment. Be patient. Be attentive to your wife's and child's needs. Work at understanding how your wife has changed now that she has become a mother. And remember the best way to build intimacy into your marriage is to help and support her in her new role as a mom. Coming alongside her will go a long way to helping both of you put your relationship first—even in the middle of parenting demands.

In parenting, what God asks of you is first and foremost to love your wife and to give up your life for her, just as Christ did for his bride, the church. As the apostle Paul says, "Husbands, love your wives, as Christ loved the church and gave himself up for her" (Ephesians 5:25). As you grow in loving your wife like this, you will also grow together to be good parents.

But perhaps you are not married to your baby's mom. No matter what the circumstances, commit yourself to treating your baby's mother with respect and care. This is always an important part of being a good dad. And remember to stay invested in your child's life, regardless of your relationship with his or her mother.

Learn to Be a Dad like Your Heavenly Father

When you think about a *good* father, who comes to mind? How do you know what a father is? What does he say? What does he do? Maybe you had a great dad, and you hope to be a lot like him. Maybe you have a more idealized view of a father, or much worse, maybe you've never seen a good example of a loving father. What should matter to a dad? What values should be personified in a father? How can you model the best of fatherhood? Where do you turn and whom should you ask to figure this out?

While looking to other dads as examples can be helpful, we fall short if we stop there. To really understand fatherhood, we have to look to our heavenly Father. How can knowing God the heavenly Father help you as an earthly dad?

The best way to see what fatherhood should really look like is to look to God. God is often described as a Father in the Bible (Deuteronomy 32:6; Isaiah 45:9–12). He is the "father to the fatherless" (Psalm 68:5), the one who formed us (Psalm 139:13–14), the one who Jesus called "Abba" or Daddy (Mark 14:36).

The greatest Father, the father of all fathers, is our heavenly Father. He gives us the ultimate picture of what true fatherhood looks like. Looking to the examples set by other fathers and reading books written by experienced dads can be helpful. Each good father gives us a glimpse of how to grow in love for our children. But as they teach us principles and tell us stories about parenting, we only get one piece of the picture of what a real father might be. The only complete picture of fatherhood comes as we look to God. True fatherhood is found in the character of the One who was willing to send his Son to die on the cross for sinners like you and me. He alone knows how to parent us perfectly. Where your parenting falls short, as it certainly will, you can look to God, who does all things well. You can depend on him to do what you can't do and to give you wisdom when you don't have any. Here are some things about God as Father that you can depend on in the days ahead:

God's Control over Our Lives

As a father, you are going to desire to control your child, or be "sovereign" in his life in a way that only God can. In your baby's first year of life you are reminded of this fact when you want the baby to do something (sleep, eat, burp, stop crying) and yet nothing you do seems to help. These moments don't happen all of the time, but they do happen and serve as a good reminder of who is really in control.

Imagine this situation: It's the middle of the night, you've fed the baby, given her a clean diaper, and she refuses to go back to sleep. Even worse, she's crying nonstop. You get this sinking feeling of doom, and a thought flashes across your mind, *I'm not in control anymore.* Those moments are good reminders that God is the baby's Lord; he is sovereign over your baby's heart and life, and you are not. This won't be the last time you have to remember that God is in control and not you. This might seem scary at first (who likes not being in control?). But when you realize that God knows what's best for you and your child, you will be able to trust him for your long parenting days and sometimes even longer nights.

God's Love

After you become a father, you will grow in your understanding of God's love for you. Parenting is a great picture of God's love for his children. Every time you pick up your crying child and hold him, it will remind you of how God cares for you (1 Peter 5:7). When your child scrapes his knee and you clean and bandage it, think about how God comforts you in your distress (2 Corinthians 1). If your child wakes you in the middle of the night, don't forget that God never sleeps, but he is watching over you day and night (Psalm 121:3–4). If your child makes a mistake, think about how God disciplines us in his love and also forgives when we ask, no matter how often we fail (Hebrews 12:7–11; 1 John 1:9–10). Thinking about all of the ways God is a perfect Father to both you and your child will fill you with thankfulness.

God's Grace

At one meeting with a mother and father, the father walked in wearing a T-shirt that said, "The Greatest Dad in the World." Whether he wore the T-shirt specifically for our meeting (we were about to talk about their parenting), or whether it was what his kids really thought about him, only the Lord knows.

You might hope to be a great dad one day. Inevitably, no matter how well prepared you are, you'll fail and make mistakes. You'll have regrets and sometimes feel at the end of yourself. Parenting is hard work. It's rewarding work, but some days it is really tough. To get through each day, you'll need to rely on God's grace.

As soon as we had our first child, I realized that no one can do this alone. The good news is that there is an unlimited supply of God's grace available to those who ask for it. God will give you grace for the transition—for the tiredness, for the short tempers, for the sleepless nights, for figuring things out, etc. You'll be tempted to be selfish when you'll need to be sacrificial; to fear when you should be courageous; to be frustrated when you should be patient. Still, God's grace will be sufficient (2 Corinthians 12:7–10). His grace will be more than enough to carry you through all the wonderful and difficult moments, and through each and every day.

It was twelve years ago when my wife first told me I was about to become a father. Now, five children later, I can testify to the fact that God's grace is truly sufficient. On difficult days you might think that survival is the goal. But with God's strength you can do more than just *survive*; you can *thrive* as a father. Fatherhood will not be through your own strength, but the strength that God provides to make it to the end of each day (Ephesians 6:10).

Practical Suggestions: Getting Ready for the Big Change

Nine months may seem like a lot of time right now, but it will go by quickly. With each passing day you'll feel the pressure of the clock ticking. Let me give you a few quick warnings, suggestions, and reminders to help you get ready.

Help your wife. More than likely, your wife's been a little sick recently. Morning sickness takes over; she is nauseous all of the time and often on the verge of throwing up. This part of the pregnancy is difficult, but sickness is a good sign because it means your baby is still growing. Even if your wife isn't sick (some women aren't), she will definitely be exhausted. So she will need more help at home. You'll need to pick up some of the slack, both now and especially after the baby arrives.

Don't be shy or stubborn about the domestic duties. Take out the trash. Do the dishes and laundry. Cook dinner. If you haven't helped like this before, consider it a practical way to show your wife that you love her. If you are wondering how to build intimacy with your wife during this difficult time, this is really the best way to start. She needs your help right now!

The most common question throughout your wife's pregnancy should be, "Anything I can do to help you?" Make sure to check with her regularly to see how you can serve her both before and after the baby arrives.

Get ready for parenthood. Ask dads you respect for fatherly advice. What lessons have they learned? What mistakes have they made? Take some time to read about parenting. Find a good book or read from sources you trust on the Internet. If your church has one, go to a parenting class. Listen to podcasts. Whatever you read, listen to, or attend, do it together with your wife so you can get on the same page about parenting. Talk with your wife about your fears, joys, and expectations. Pray for your baby with her. Pray for a healthy child and for the Lord to sustain your wife, but also begin to pray for your child to know God's love. If you don't do anything to prepare for becoming a parent, you'll parent like your parents did. For some of us that may be a good thing, but for many of us it is not.

Stay involved. Your wife and the baby are going through a very special bonding time during the pregnancy and beyond. Don't drift into the background. Just because she's more excited about the baby than she is about you right now doesn't mean you should find some convenient distraction (e.g., work more hours or find a new hobby). The more you get involved in the pregnancy, the more you'll feel connected to the baby. After all, this is your child too.

Expect your sex life to change. Sometimes it starts in pregnancy. Your wife is sick so sex slows down. As the pregnancy progresses, sex can be awkward. After the baby comes, she'll need to recover (and recovery is longer after a C-section). Since the baby is up at all hours of the night, you'll both desperately want sleep, but you will (secretly) yearn to be intimate with her. In the midst of all this, you'll miss her more. Don't worry, eventually intimacy will come back. One more way to help your wife through this time is by accepting that this is a difficult season for intimacy and not pressuring her to be intimate when she is not ready for it.

Rework your family budget. She may not be able to work, especially if she or the baby gets sick. And you'll have to buy a lot of baby stuff along the way. So go back to your budget and rework the numbers.

Make space for the baby. Get ready for the stuff. Babies need a lot of it—clothes, car seat, diapers, wipes, burp cloths, pacifiers, crib, feeding chair, changing table, to name just a few items. And depending on the size of your place, you'll need to reorganize in order to make room for the baby. You'll want to repaint the new baby room, get a crib and a changing table set up, and anything else to make it cozy for your baby.

Have a babymoon. Before the little one comes, get away with your wife. Get some quality time together. Your marriage does matter so take some time to invest in it before the big transition hits.

Before the baby arrives, get on the same page about visitors. Some couples want their family around soon after the birth. Some couples need a little space before family or friends start their invasion. Make sure you talk to your wife about her desires before the baby comes. Does she want her parents around? When can your family see the child? What if her friends from church or work ask about coming over? Answer these questions *now* rather than on the spur of the moment after the baby is born.

Marvel at the miraculous birth. The first time I saw my wife deliver a baby, I was speechless. Very few things in my life fit in the category of a miracle, but childbirth certainly does. The moment is breathtaking. When my wife got pregnant with our second child, I approached the birth with the attitude "Been there, done that." But I was wrong! The second birth was just as miraculous and wondrous as the first.

Starting off as new parents. Several days after the birth, as I pulled our car to the side door of the hospital, a nurse wheeled my wife and newborn son up to the car and helped them both in. After walking alongside of us to get us through the birthing process and help us make the first adjustments to parenthood, the nurse dropped us off at our car, wished us well, and walked away. Looking back at our son, my wife commented, "I can't believe that it is up to us to raise him." As you begin parenthood, you suddenly realize that this precious life is now *your* responsibility, and as scary as it is becoming first-time parents, it is a good responsibility to take on. Keep in mind that you are not alone. God is with you. He will help you figure it out. His mercy and grace are available in abundance to help you learn how to be a good parent.

Be prepared for sleep deprivation. You'll have less sleep in general and some sleepless nights. It's incredible how one little person can cause so much exhaustion. Talk with your wife about how you can help her get rest, whether it's by staying up with the baby at night or making sure she is able to nap during the day. It's your job to make sure she rests as much as possible and doesn't feel a lot of pressure to take care of stuff around the house. Pick up the slack wherever possible so that she is able to rest.

Expect less time alone. Once your baby arrives, you might feel like you rarely get time alone with your wife. You'll miss uninterrupted time with your best friend. Date nights and long conversations will come back one day. But for now you'll need to be patient as you work together through the transition.

Treat your baby with respect. From the very beginning, treat your child with the dignity that an image-bearer deserves (Genesis 1:26–28). Be like the young father, who upon arriving home for the first time with his wife and child, walked around the apartment giving his newborn son a tour of their place. "This room is the kitchen, where Mommy and I will make your meals . . . and over here is the living room, where you and I will watch NFL games . . . and this is your room with your new crib . . . " A guided tour for a baby might seem silly, but in some sense, this father understood the respect that every child deserves.

Know that eventually your family will settle at a new norm. Every family has its own rhythm that defines the pace of life. When the baby arrives, that rhythm is thrown off for a time. But after a few months the family settles in at a new norm. Having a baby in the home becomes natural.

Adjust your expectations. Don't assume that you will be able to do everything in the same ways that you did before. You will need to adjust your expectations, and the expectations of your family and friends, about what travel, hospitality, time hanging out, etc. will look like after the baby is born. Don't make any major commitments *before* the baby is born that would hinder your ability to serve your family *after* the baby is born. Once you have settled into a new normal, post-baby, you can reevaluate your commitments and decide what would be wise to take back.

Through all the hard work as a parent, there can be some very long days. My wife once said to me, "A day feels like forever, but the years fly by." Right now you might feel like the biggest thing you have to deal with is getting used to being a father, but you'll turn around one day and be surprised. Your baby will have grown up and become a teenager (or a college student, or a full-grown adult)! And you'll say, "What happened?" Don't ever take for granted the time you have with your children. Cherish every moment. Take advantage of every opportunity to engage, pour into, and love your family. In the end the one thing you will never regret is your investment in your children.

I've been a father for many years now. There have been plenty of good days and bad days. But through it all, our heavenly Father has remained faithful to my family. Because God has been faithful in the past, I can look to the future with confidence that he will remain the same—present, faithful, forgiving, and loving to me, my wife, and my five children (1 Thessalonians 5:24). Twelve years into my parenting journey, with many years left to go, I am so thankful to my faithful God who gives grace in abundance to those who do not deserve it.

Simple, Quick, Biblical

Advice on Complicated Counseling Issues
for Pastors, Counselors, and Individuals

MINIBOOK
CATEGORIES

- Personal Change
- Marriage & Parenting
- Medical & Psychiatric Issues
- Women's Issues
- Singles
- Military

USE YOURSELF | GIVE TO A FRIEND | DISPLAY IN YOUR CHURCH OR MINISTRY

New Growth Press

Go to www.newgrowthpress.com or call 336.378.7775 to
purchase individual minibooks or the entire collection.
Durable acrylic display stands are also available to house
the minibook collection.